Geocaching

Log Book

2
Geocaching

Geocaching
Log Book

Copyright © 2008 by Michael Sajdak

Published by
www.createspace.com

Cache Name	
Cache#	
Coordinates Lat	
Coordinates Lon	
Date Found	
Notes	
Hints	
Comments	

Cache Name	
Cache#	
Coordinates Lat	
Coordinates Lon	
Date Found	
Notes	
Hints	
Comments	

Decryption Key

A	B	C	D	E	F	G	H	I	J	K	L	M
N	O	P	Q	R	S	T	U	V	W	X	Y	Z

(letter above equals below, and vice versa)

Cache Name	
Cache#	
Coordinates Lat	
Coordinates Lon	
Date Found	
Notes	
Hints	
Comments	

Cache Name	
Cache#	
Coordinates Lat	
Coordinates Lon	
Date Found	
Notes	
Hints	
Comments	

Decryption Key

A	B	C	D	E	F	G	H	I	J	K	L	M
N	O	P	Q	R	S	T	U	V	W	X	Y	Z

(letter above equals below, and vice versa)

Cache Name	
Cache#	
Coordinates Lat	
Coordinates Lon	
Date Found	
Notes	
Hints	
Comments	

Cache Name	
Cache#	
Coordinates Lat	
Coordinates Lon	
Date Found	
Notes	
Hints	
Comments	

Decryption Key

A	B	C	D	E	F	G	H	I	J	K	L	M
N	O	P	Q	R	S	T	U	V	W	X	Y	Z

(letter above equals below, and vice versa)

Cache Name	
Cache#	
Coordinates Lat	
Coordinates Lon	
Date Found	
Notes	
Hints	
Comments	

Cache Name	
Cache#	
Coordinates Lat	
Coordinates Lon	
Date Found	
Notes	
Hints	
Comments	

Decryption Key

A	B	C	D	E	F	G	H	I	J	K	L	M
N	O	P	Q	R	S	T	U	V	W	X	Y	Z

(letter above equals below, and vice versa)

Cache Name	
Cache#	
Coordinates Lat	
Coordinates Lon	
Date Found	
Notes	
Hints	
Comments	

Cache Name	
Cache#	
Coordinates Lat	
Coordinates Lon	
Date Found	
Notes	
Hints	
Comments	

Decryption Key

A	B	C	D	E	F	G	H	I	J	K	L	M
N	O	P	Q	R	S	T	U	V	W	X	Y	Z

(letter above equals below, and vice versa)

Cache Name	
Cache#	
Coordinates Lat	
Coordinates Lon	
Date Found	
Notes	
Hints	
Comments	

Cache Name	
Cache#	
Coordinates Lat	
Coordinates Lon	
Date Found	
Notes	
Hints	
Comments	

Decryption Key

A	B	C	D	E	F	G	H	I	J	K	L	M
N	O	P	Q	R	S	T	U	V	W	X	Y	Z

(letter above equals below, and vice versa)

Cache Name	
Cache#	
Coordinates Lat	
Coordinates Lon	
Date Found	
Notes	
Hints	
Comments	

Cache Name	
Cache#	
Coordinates Lat	
Coordinates Lon	
Date Found	
Notes	
Hints	
Comments	

Decryption Key

A	B	C	D	E	F	G	H	I	J	K	L	M
N	O	P	Q	R	S	T	U	V	W	X	Y	Z

(letter above equals below, and vice versa)

Cache Name	
Cache#	
Coordinates Lat	
Coordinates Lon	
Date Found	
Notes	
Hints	
Comments	

Cache Name	
Cache#	
Coordinates Lat	
Coordinates Lon	
Date Found	
Notes	
Hints	
Comments	

Decryption Key

A	B	C	D	E	F	G	H	I	J	K	L	M
N	O	P	Q	R	S	T	U	V	W	X	Y	Z

(letter above equals below, and vice versa)

Cache Name	
Cache#	
Coordinates Lat	
Coordinates Lon	
Date Found	
Notes	
Hints	
Comments	

Cache Name	
Cache#	
Coordinates Lat	
Coordinates Lon	
Date Found	
Notes	
Hints	
Comments	

Decryption Key

A	B	C	D	E	F	G	H	I	J	K	L	M
N	O	P	Q	R	S	T	U	V	W	X	Y	Z

(letter above equals below, and vice versa)

Cache Name	
Cache#	
Coordinates Lat	
Coordinates Lon	
Date Found	
Notes	
Hints	
Comments	

Cache Name	
Cache#	
Coordinates Lat	
Coordinates Lon	
Date Found	
Notes	
Hints	
Comments	

Decryption Key

A	B	C	D	E	F	G	H	I	J	K	L	M
N	O	P	Q	R	S	T	U	V	W	X	Y	Z

(letter above equals below, and vice versa)

Cache Name	
Cache#	
Coordinates Lat	
Coordinates Lon	
Date Found	
Notes	
Hints	
Comments	

Cache Name	
Cache#	
Coordinates Lat	
Coordinates Lon	
Date Found	
Notes	
Hints	
Comments	

Decryption Key

A	B	C	D	E	F	G	H	I	J	K	L	M
N	O	P	Q	R	S	T	U	V	W	X	Y	Z

(letter above equals below, and vice versa)

Cache Name	
Cache#	
Coordinates Lat	
Coordinates Lon	
Date Found	
Notes	
Hints	
Comments	

Cache Name	
Cache#	
Coordinates Lat	
Coordinates Lon	
Date Found	
Notes	
Hints	
Comments	

Decryption Key

A	B	C	D	E	F	G	H	I	J	K	L	M
N	O	P	Q	R	S	T	U	V	W	X	Y	Z

(letter above equals below, and vice versa)

Cache Name	
Cache#	
Coordinates Lat	
Coordinates Lon	
Date Found	
Notes	
Hints	
Comments	

Cache Name	
Cache#	
Coordinates Lat	
Coordinates Lon	
Date Found	
Notes	
Hints	
Comments	

Decryption Key

A	B	C	D	E	F	G	H	I	J	K	L	M
N	O	P	Q	R	S	T	U	V	W	X	Y	Z

(letter above equals below, and vice versa)

Cache Name	
Cache#	
Coordinates Lat	
Coordinates Lon	
Date Found	
Notes	
Hints	
Comments	

Cache Name	
Cache#	
Coordinates Lat	
Coordinates Lon	
Date Found	
Notes	
Hints	
Comments	

Decryption Key

A	B	C	D	E	F	G	H	I	J	K	L	M
N	O	P	Q	R	S	T	U	V	W	X	Y	Z

(letter above equals below, and vice versa)

Cache Name	
Cache#	
Coordinates Lat	
Coordinates Lon	
Date Found	
Notes	
Hints	
Comments	

Cache Name	
Cache#	
Coordinates Lat	
Coordinates Lon	
Date Found	
Notes	
Hints	
Comments	

Decryption Key

A	B	C	D	E	F	G	H	I	J	K	L	M
N	O	P	Q	R	S	T	U	V	W	X	Y	Z

(letter above equals below, and vice versa)

Cache Name	
Cache#	
Coordinates Lat	
Coordinates Lon	
Date Found	
Notes	
Hints	
Comments	

Cache Name	
Cache#	
Coordinates Lat	
Coordinates Lon	
Date Found	
Notes	
Hints	
Comments	

Decryption Key

A	B	C	D	E	F	G	H	I	J	K	L	M
N	O	P	Q	R	S	T	U	V	W	X	Y	Z

(letter above equals below, and vice versa)

Cache Name	
Cache#	
Coordinates Lat	
Coordinates Lon	
Date Found	
Notes	
Hints	
Comments	

Cache Name	
Cache#	
Coordinates Lat	
Coordinates Lon	
Date Found	
Notes	
Hints	
Comments	

Decryption Key

A	B	C	D	E	F	G	H	I	J	K	L	M
N	O	P	Q	R	S	T	U	V	W	X	Y	Z

(letter above equals below, and vice versa)

Cache Name	
Cache#	
Coordinates Lat	
Coordinates Lon	
Date Found	
Notes	
Hints	
Comments	

Cache Name	
Cache#	
Coordinates Lat	
Coordinates Lon	
Date Found	
Notes	
Hints	
Comments	

Decryption Key

A	B	C	D	E	F	G	H	I	J	K	L	M
N	O	P	Q	R	S	T	U	V	W	X	Y	Z

(letter above equals below, and vice versa)

Cache Name	
Cache#	
Coordinates Lat	
Coordinates Lon	
Date Found	
Notes	
Hints	
Comments	

Cache Name	
Cache#	
Coordinates Lat	
Coordinates Lon	
Date Found	
Notes	
Hints	
Comments	

Decryption Key

A	B	C	D	E	F	G	H	I	J	K	L	M
N	O	P	Q	R	S	T	U	V	W	X	Y	Z

(letter above equals below, and vice versa)

Cache Name	
Cache#	
Coordinates Lat	
Coordinates Lon	
Date Found	
Notes	
Hints	
Comments	

Cache Name	
Cache#	
Coordinates Lat	
Coordinates Lon	
Date Found	
Notes	
Hints	
Comments	

Decryption Key

A	B	C	D	E	F	G	H	I	J	K	L	M
N	O	P	Q	R	S	T	U	V	W	X	Y	Z

(letter above equals below, and vice versa)

Cache Name	
Cache#	
Coordinates Lat	
Coordinates Lon	
Date Found	
Notes	
Hints	
Comments	

Cache Name	
Cache#	
Coordinates Lat	
Coordinates Lon	
Date Found	
Notes	
Hints	
Comments	

Decryption Key

A	B	C	D	E	F	G	H	I	J	K	L	M
N	O	P	Q	R	S	T	U	V	W	X	Y	Z

(letter above equals below, and vice versa)

Geocaching

Cache Name	
Cache#	
Coordinates Lat	
Coordinates Lon	
Date Found	
Notes	
Hints	
Comments	

Cache Name	
Cache#	
Coordinates Lat	
Coordinates Lon	
Date Found	
Notes	
Hints	
Comments	

Decryption Key

A	B	C	D	E	F	G	H	I	J	K	L	M
N	O	P	Q	R	S	T	U	V	W	X	Y	Z

(letter above equals below, and vice versa)

Cache Name	
Cache#	
Coordinates Lat	
Coordinates Lon	
Date Found	
Notes	
Hints	
Comments	

Cache Name	
Cache#	
Coordinates Lat	
Coordinates Lon	
Date Found	
Notes	
Hints	
Comments	

Decryption Key

A	B	C	D	E	F	G	H	I	J	K	L	M
N	O	P	Q	R	S	T	U	V	W	X	Y	Z

(letter above equals below, and vice versa)

Geocaching

Cache Name	
Cache#	
Coordinates Lat	
Coordinates Lon	
Date Found	
Notes	
Hints	
Comments	

Cache Name	
Cache#	
Coordinates Lat	
Coordinates Lon	
Date Found	
Notes	
Hints	
Comments	

Decryption Key

A	B	C	D	E	F	G	H	I	J	K	L	M
N	O	P	Q	R	S	T	U	V	W	X	Y	Z

(letter above equals below, and vice versa)

Cache Name	
Cache#	
Coordinates Lat	
Coordinates Lon	
Date Found	
Notes	
Hints	
Comments	

Cache Name	
Cache#	
Coordinates Lat	
Coordinates Lon	
Date Found	
Notes	
Hints	
Comments	

Decryption Key

A	B	C	D	E	F	G	H	I	J	K	L	M
N	O	P	Q	R	S	T	U	V	W	X	Y	Z

(letter above equals below, and vice versa)

Cache Name	
Cache#	
Coordinates Lat	
Coordinates Lon	
Date Found	
Notes	
Hints	
Comments	

Cache Name	
Cache#	
Coordinates Lat	
Coordinates Lon	
Date Found	
Notes	
Hints	
Comments	

Decryption Key

A	B	C	D	E	F	G	H	I	J	K	L	M
N	O	P	Q	R	S	T	U	V	W	X	Y	Z

(letter above equals below, and vice versa)

Cache Name	
Cache#	
Coordinates Lat	
Coordinates Lon	
Date Found	
Notes	
Hints	
Comments	

Cache Name	
Cache#	
Coordinates Lat	
Coordinates Lon	
Date Found	
Notes	
Hints	
Comments	

Decryption Key

A	B	C	D	E	F	G	H	I	J	K	L	M
N	O	P	Q	R	S	T	U	V	W	X	Y	Z

(letter above equals below, and vice versa)

Cache Name	
Cache#	
Coordinates Lat	
Coordinates Lon	
Date Found	
Notes	
Hints	
Comments	

Cache Name	
Cache#	
Coordinates Lat	
Coordinates Lon	
Date Found	
Notes	
Hints	
Comments	

Decryption Key

A	B	C	D	E	F	G	H	I	J	K	L	M
N	O	P	Q	R	S	T	U	V	W	X	Y	Z

(letter above equals below, and vice versa)

Cache Name	
Cache#	
Coordinates Lat	
Coordinates Lon	
Date Found	
Notes	
Hints	
Comments	

Cache Name	
Cache#	
Coordinates Lat	
Coordinates Lon	
Date Found	
Notes	
Hints	
Comments	

Decryption Key

A	B	C	D	E	F	G	H	I	J	K	L	M
N	O	P	Q	R	S	T	U	V	W	X	Y	Z

(letter above equals below, and vice versa)

Cache Name	
Cache#	
Coordinates Lat	
Coordinates Lon	
Date Found	
Notes	
Hints	
Comments	

Cache Name	
Cache#	
Coordinates Lat	
Coordinates Lon	
Date Found	
Notes	
Hints	
Comments	

Decryption Key

A	B	C	D	E	F	G	H	I	J	K	L	M
N	O	P	Q	R	S	T	U	V	W	X	Y	Z

(letter above equals below, and vice versa)

Cache Name	
Cache#	
Coordinates Lat	
Coordinates Lon	
Date Found	
Notes	
Hints	
Comments	

Cache Name	
Cache#	
Coordinates Lat	
Coordinates Lon	
Date Found	
Notes	
Hints	
Comments	

Decryption Key

A	B	C	D	E	F	G	H	I	J	K	L	M
N	O	P	Q	R	S	T	U	V	W	X	Y	Z

(letter above equals below, and vice versa)

Cache Name	
Cache#	
Coordinates Lat	
Coordinates Lon	
Date Found	
Notes	
Hints	
Comments	

Cache Name	
Cache#	
Coordinates Lat	
Coordinates Lon	
Date Found	
Notes	
Hints	
Comments	

Decryption Key

A	B	C	D	E	F	G	H	I	J	K	L	M
N	O	P	Q	R	S	T	U	V	W	X	Y	Z

(letter above equals below, and vice versa)

Cache Name	
Cache#	
Coordinates Lat	
Coordinates Lon	
Date Found	
Notes	
Hints	
Comments	

Cache Name	
Cache#	
Coordinates Lat	
Coordinates Lon	
Date Found	
Notes	
Hints	
Comments	

Decryption Key

A	B	C	D	E	F	G	H	I	J	K	L	M
N	O	P	Q	R	S	T	U	V	W	X	Y	Z

(letter above equals below, and vice versa)

Cache Name	
Cache#	
Coordinates Lat	
Coordinates Lon	
Date Found	
Notes	
Hints	
Comments	

Cache Name	
Cache#	
Coordinates Lat	
Coordinates Lon	
Date Found	
Notes	
Hints	
Comments	

Decryption Key

A	B	C	D	E	F	G	H	I	J	K	L	M
N	O	P	Q	R	S	T	U	V	W	X	Y	Z

(letter above equals below, and vice versa)

Cache Name	
Cache#	
Coordinates Lat	
Coordinates Lon	
Date Found	
Notes	
Hints	
Comments	

Cache Name	
Cache#	
Coordinates Lat	
Coordinates Lon	
Date Found	
Notes	
Hints	
Comments	

Decryption Key

A	B	C	D	E	F	G	H	I	J	K	L	M
N	O	P	Q	R	S	T	U	V	W	X	Y	Z

(letter above equals below, and vice versa)

Cache Name	
Cache#	
Coordinates Lat	
Coordinates Lon	
Date Found	
Notes	
Hints	
Comments	

Cache Name	
Cache#	
Coordinates Lat	
Coordinates Lon	
Date Found	
Notes	
Hints	
Comments	

Decryption Key

A	B	C	D	E	F	G	H	I	J	K	L	M
N	O	P	Q	R	S	T	U	V	W	X	Y	Z

(letter above equals below, and vice versa)

Cache Name	
Cache#	
Coordinates Lat	
Coordinates Lon	
Date Found	
Notes	
Hints	
Comments	

Cache Name	
Cache#	
Coordinates Lat	
Coordinates Lon	
Date Found	
Notes	
Hints	
Comments	

Decryption Key

A	B	C	D	E	F	G	H	I	J	K	L	M
N	O	P	Q	R	S	T	U	V	W	X	Y	Z

(letter above equals below, and vice versa)

Cache Name	
Cache#	
Coordinates Lat	
Coordinates Lon	
Date Found	
Notes	
Hints	
Comments	

Cache Name	
Cache#	
Coordinates Lat	
Coordinates Lon	
Date Found	
Notes	
Hints	
Comments	

Decryption Key

A	B	C	D	E	F	G	H	I	J	K	L	M
N	O	P	Q	R	S	T	U	V	W	X	Y	Z

(letter above equals below, and vice versa)

Cache Name	
Cache#	
Coordinates Lat	
Coordinates Lon	
Date Found	
Notes	
Hints	
Comments	

Cache Name	
Cache#	
Coordinates Lat	
Coordinates Lon	
Date Found	
Notes	
Hints	
Comments	

Decryption Key

A	B	C	D	E	F	G	H	I	J	K	L	M
N	O	P	Q	R	S	T	U	V	W	X	Y	Z

(letter above equals below, and vice versa)

Cache Name	
Cache#	
Coordinates Lat	
Coordinates Lon	
Date Found	
Notes	
Hints	
Comments	

Cache Name	
Cache#	
Coordinates Lat	
Coordinates Lon	
Date Found	
Notes	
Hints	
Comments	

Decryption Key

A	B	C	D	E	F	G	H	I	J	K	L	M
N	O	P	Q	R	S	T	U	V	W	X	Y	Z

(letter above equals below, and vice versa)

Cache Name	
Cache#	
Coordinates Lat	
Coordinates Lon	
Date Found	
Notes	
Hints	
Comments	

Cache Name	
Cache#	
Coordinates Lat	
Coordinates Lon	
Date Found	
Notes	
Hints	
Comments	

Decryption Key

A	B	C	D	E	F	G	H	I	J	K	L	M
N	O	P	Q	R	S	T	U	V	W	X	Y	Z

(letter above equals below, and vice versa)

Cache Name	
Cache#	
Coordinates Lat	
Coordinates Lon	
Date Found	
Notes	
Hints	
Comments	

Cache Name	
Cache#	
Coordinates Lat	
Coordinates Lon	
Date Found	
Notes	
Hints	
Comments	

Decryption Key

A	B	C	D	E	F	G	H	I	J	K	L	M
N	O	P	Q	R	S	T	U	V	W	X	Y	Z

(letter above equals below, and vice versa)

Cache Name	
Cache#	
Coordinates Lat	
Coordinates Lon	
Date Found	
Notes	
Hints	
Comments	

Cache Name	
Cache#	
Coordinates Lat	
Coordinates Lon	
Date Found	
Notes	
Hints	
Comments	

Decryption Key

A	B	C	D	E	F	G	H	I	J	K	L	M
N	O	P	Q	R	S	T	U	V	W	X	Y	Z

(letter above equals below, and vice versa)

Cache Name	
Cache#	
Coordinates Lat	
Coordinates Lon	
Date Found	
Notes	
Hints	
Comments	

Cache Name	
Cache#	
Coordinates Lat	
Coordinates Lon	
Date Found	
Notes	
Hints	
Comments	

Decryption Key

A	B	C	D	E	F	G	H	I	J	K	L	M
N	O	P	Q	R	S	T	U	V	W	X	Y	Z

(letter above equals below, and vice versa)

Cache Name	
Cache#	
Coordinates Lat	
Coordinates Lon	
Date Found	
Notes	
Hints	
Comments	

Cache Name	
Cache#	
Coordinates Lat	
Coordinates Lon	
Date Found	
Notes	
Hints	
Comments	

Decryption Key

A	B	C	D	E	F	G	H	I	J	K	L	M
N	O	P	Q	R	S	T	U	V	W	X	Y	Z

(letter above equals below, and vice versa)

Cache Name	
Cache#	
Coordinates Lat	
Coordinates Lon	
Date Found	
Notes	
Hints	
Comments	

Cache Name	
Cache#	
Coordinates Lat	
Coordinates Lon	
Date Found	
Notes	
Hints	
Comments	

Decryption Key

A	B	C	D	E	F	G	H	I	J	K	L	M
N	O	P	Q	R	S	T	U	V	W	X	Y	Z

(letter above equals below, and vice versa)

Cache Name	
Cache#	
Coordinates Lat	
Coordinates Lon	
Date Found	
Notes	
Hints	
Comments	

Cache Name	
Cache#	
Coordinates Lat	
Coordinates Lon	
Date Found	
Notes	
Hints	
Comments	

Decryption Key

A	B	C	D	E	F	G	H	I	J	K	L	M
N	O	P	Q	R	S	T	U	V	W	X	Y	Z

(letter above equals below, and vice versa)

Cache Name	
Cache#	
Coordinates Lat	
Coordinates Lon	
Date Found	
Notes	
Hints	
Comments	

Cache Name	
Cache#	
Coordinates Lat	
Coordinates Lon	
Date Found	
Notes	
Hints	
Comments	

Decryption Key

A	B	C	D	E	F	G	H	I	J	K	L	M
N	O	P	Q	R	S	T	U	V	W	X	Y	Z

(letter above equals below, and vice versa)

Cache Name	
Cache#	
Coordinates Lat	
Coordinates Lon	
Date Found	
Notes	
Hints	
Comments	

Cache Name	
Cache#	
Coordinates Lat	
Coordinates Lon	
Date Found	
Notes	
Hints	
Comments	

Decryption Key

A	B	C	D	E	F	G	H	I	J	K	L	M
N	O	P	Q	R	S	T	U	V	W	X	Y	Z

(letter above equals below, and vice versa)

Cache Name	
Cache#	
Coordinates Lat	
Coordinates Lon	
Date Found	
Notes	
Hints	
Comments	

Cache Name	
Cache#	
Coordinates Lat	
Coordinates Lon	
Date Found	
Notes	
Hints	
Comments	

Decryption Key

A	B	C	D	E	F	G	H	I	J	K	L	M
N	O	P	Q	R	S	T	U	V	W	X	Y	Z

(letter above equals below, and vice versa)

Cache Name	
Cache#	
Coordinates Lat	
Coordinates Lon	
Date Found	
Notes	
Hints	
Comments	

Cache Name	
Cache#	
Coordinates Lat	
Coordinates Lon	
Date Found	
Notes	
Hints	
Comments	

Decryption Key

A	B	C	D	E	F	G	H	I	J	K	L	M
N	O	P	Q	R	S	T	U	V	W	X	Y	Z

(letter above equals below, and vice versa)

Cache Name	
Cache#	
Coordinates Lat	
Coordinates Lon	
Date Found	
Notes	
Hints	
Comments	

Cache Name	
Cache#	
Coordinates Lat	
Coordinates Lon	
Date Found	
Notes	
Hints	
Comments	

Decryption Key

A	B	C	D	E	F	G	H	I	J	K	L	M
N	O	P	Q	R	S	T	U	V	W	X	Y	Z

(letter above equals below, and vice versa)

Cache Name	
Cache#	
Coordinates Lat	
Coordinates Lon	
Date Found	
Notes	
Hints	
Comments	

Cache Name	
Cache#	
Coordinates Lat	
Coordinates Lon	
Date Found	
Notes	
Hints	
Comments	

Decryption Key

A	B	C	D	E	F	G	H	I	J	K	L	M
N	O	P	Q	R	S	T	U	V	W	X	Y	Z

(letter above equals below, and vice versa)

Cache Name	
Cache#	
Coordinates Lat	
Coordinates Lon	
Date Found	
Notes	
Hints	
Comments	

Cache Name	
Cache#	
Coordinates Lat	
Coordinates Lon	
Date Found	
Notes	
Hints	
Comments	

Decryption Key

A	B	C	D	E	F	G	H	I	J	K	L	M
N	O	P	Q	R	S	T	U	V	W	X	Y	Z

(letter above equals below, and vice versa)

Cache Name	
Cache#	
Coordinates Lat	
Coordinates Lon	
Date Found	
Notes	
Hints	
Comments	

Cache Name	
Cache#	
Coordinates Lat	
Coordinates Lon	
Date Found	
Notes	
Hints	
Comments	

Decryption Key

A	B	C	D	E	F	G	H	I	J	K	L	M
N	O	P	Q	R	S	T	U	V	W	X	Y	Z

(letter above equals below, and vice versa)

Cache Name	
Cache#	
Coordinates Lat	
Coordinates Lon	
Date Found	
Notes	
Hints	
Comments	

Cache Name	
Cache#	
Coordinates Lat	
Coordinates Lon	
Date Found	
Notes	
Hints	
Comments	

Decryption Key

A	B	C	D	E	F	G	H	I	J	K	L	M
N	O	P	Q	R	S	T	U	V	W	X	Y	Z

(letter above equals below, and vice versa)

Cache Name	
Cache#	
Coordinates Lat	
Coordinates Lon	
Date Found	
Notes	
Hints	
Comments	

Cache Name	
Cache#	
Coordinates Lat	
Coordinates Lon	
Date Found	
Notes	
Hints	
Comments	

Decryption Key

A	B	C	D	E	F	G	H	I	J	K	L	M
N	O	P	Q	R	S	T	U	V	W	X	Y	Z

(letter above equals below, and vice versa)

Cache Name	
Cache#	
Coordinates Lat	
Coordinates Lon	
Date Found	
Notes	
Hints	
Comments	

Cache Name	
Cache#	
Coordinates Lat	
Coordinates Lon	
Date Found	
Notes	
Hints	
Comments	

Decryption Key

A	B	C	D	E	F	G	H	I	J	K	L	M
N	O	P	Q	R	S	T	U	V	W	X	Y	Z

(letter above equals below, and vice versa)

Cache Name	
Cache#	
Coordinates Lat	
Coordinates Lon	
Date Found	
Notes	
Hints	
Comments	

Cache Name	
Cache#	
Coordinates Lat	
Coordinates Lon	
Date Found	
Notes	
Hints	
Comments	

Decryption Key

A	B	C	D	E	F	G	H	I	J	K	L	M
N	O	P	Q	R	S	T	U	V	W	X	Y	Z

(letter above equals below, and vice versa)

Cache Name	
Cache#	
Coordinates Lat	
Coordinates Lon	
Date Found	
Notes	
Hints	
Comments	

Cache Name	
Cache#	
Coordinates Lat	
Coordinates Lon	
Date Found	
Notes	
Hints	
Comments	

Decryption Key

A	B	C	D	E	F	G	H	I	J	K	L	M
N	O	P	Q	R	S	T	U	V	W	X	Y	Z

(letter above equals below, and vice versa)

Cache Name	
Cache#	
Coordinates Lat	
Coordinates Lon	
Date Found	
Notes	
Hints	
Comments	

Cache Name	
Cache#	
Coordinates Lat	
Coordinates Lon	
Date Found	
Notes	
Hints	
Comments	

Decryption Key

A	B	C	D	E	F	G	H	I	J	K	L	M
N	O	P	Q	R	S	T	U	V	W	X	Y	Z

(letter above equals below, and vice versa)

Cache Name	
Cache#	
Coordinates Lat	
Coordinates Lon	
Date Found	
Notes	
Hints	
Comments	

Cache Name	
Cache#	
Coordinates Lat	
Coordinates Lon	
Date Found	
Notes	
Hints	
Comments	

Decryption Key

A	B	C	D	E	F	G	H	I	J	K	L	M
N	O	P	Q	R	S	T	U	V	W	X	Y	Z

(letter above equals below, and vice versa)

Cache Name	
Cache#	
Coordinates Lat	
Coordinates Lon	
Date Found	
Notes	
Hints	
Comments	

Cache Name	
Cache#	
Coordinates Lat	
Coordinates Lon	
Date Found	
Notes	
Hints	
Comments	

Decryption Key

A	B	C	D	E	F	G	H	I	J	K	L	M
N	O	P	Q	R	S	T	U	V	W	X	Y	Z

(letter above equals below, and vice versa)

Cache Name	
Cache#	
Coordinates Lat	
Coordinates Lon	
Date Found	
Notes	
Hints	
Comments	

Cache Name	
Cache#	
Coordinates Lat	
Coordinates Lon	
Date Found	
Notes	
Hints	
Comments	

Decryption Key

A	B	C	D	E	F	G	H	I	J	K	L	M
N	O	P	Q	R	S	T	U	V	W	X	Y	Z

(letter above equals below, and vice versa)

Cache Name	
Cache#	
Coordinates Lat	
Coordinates Lon	
Date Found	
Notes	
Hints	
Comments	

Cache Name	
Cache#	
Coordinates Lat	
Coordinates Lon	
Date Found	
Notes	
Hints	
Comments	

Decryption Key

A	B	C	D	E	F	G	H	I	J	K	L	M
N	O	P	Q	R	S	T	U	V	W	X	Y	Z

(letter above equals below, and vice versa)

Cache Name	
Cache#	
Coordinates Lat	
Coordinates Lon	
Date Found	
Notes	
Hints	
Comments	

Cache Name	
Cache#	
Coordinates Lat	
Coordinates Lon	
Date Found	
Notes	
Hints	
Comments	

Decryption Key

A	B	C	D	E	F	G	H	I	J	K	L	M
N	O	P	Q	R	S	T	U	V	W	X	Y	Z

(letter above equals below, and vice versa)

Cache Name	
Cache#	
Coordinates Lat	
Coordinates Lon	
Date Found	
Notes	
Hints	
Comments	

Cache Name	
Cache#	
Coordinates Lat	
Coordinates Lon	
Date Found	
Notes	
Hints	
Comments	

Decryption Key

A	B	C	D	E	F	G	H	I	J	K	L	M
N	O	P	Q	R	S	T	U	V	W	X	Y	Z

(letter above equals below, and vice versa)

Cache Name	
Cache#	
Coordinates Lat	
Coordinates Lon	
Date Found	
Notes	
Hints	
Comments	

Cache Name	
Cache#	
Coordinates Lat	
Coordinates Lon	
Date Found	
Notes	
Hints	
Comments	

Decryption Key

A	B	C	D	E	F	G	H	I	J	K	L	M
N	O	P	Q	R	S	T	U	V	W	X	Y	Z

(letter above equals below, and vice versa)

Cache Name	
Cache#	
Coordinates Lat	
Coordinates Lon	
Date Found	
Notes	
Hints	
Comments	

Cache Name	
Cache#	
Coordinates Lat	
Coordinates Lon	
Date Found	
Notes	
Hints	
Comments	

Decryption Key

A	B	C	D	E	F	G	H	I	J	K	L	M
N	O	P	Q	R	S	T	U	V	W	X	Y	Z

(letter above equals below, and vice versa)

Cache Name	
Cache#	
Coordinates Lat	
Coordinates Lon	
Date Found	
Notes	
Hints	
Comments	

Cache Name	
Cache#	
Coordinates Lat	
Coordinates Lon	
Date Found	
Notes	
Hints	
Comments	

Decryption Key

A	B	C	D	E	F	G	H	I	J	K	L	M
N	O	P	Q	R	S	T	U	V	W	X	Y	Z

(letter above equals below, and vice versa)

Cache Name	
Cache#	
Coordinates Lat	
Coordinates Lon	
Date Found	
Notes	
Hints	
Comments	

Cache Name	
Cache#	
Coordinates Lat	
Coordinates Lon	
Date Found	
Notes	
Hints	
Comments	

Decryption Key

A	B	C	D	E	F	G	H	I	J	K	L	M
N	O	P	Q	R	S	T	U	V	W	X	Y	Z

(letter above equals below, and vice versa)

Cache Name	
Cache#	
Coordinates Lat	
Coordinates Lon	
Date Found	
Notes	
Hints	
Comments	

Cache Name	
Cache#	
Coordinates Lat	
Coordinates Lon	
Date Found	
Notes	
Hints	
Comments	

Decryption Key

A	B	C	D	E	F	G	H	I	J	K	L	M
N	O	P	Q	R	S	T	U	V	W	X	Y	Z

(letter above equals below, and vice versa)

Cache Name	
Cache#	
Coordinates Lat	
Coordinates Lon	
Date Found	
Notes	
Hints	
Comments	

Cache Name	
Cache#	
Coordinates Lat	
Coordinates Lon	
Date Found	
Notes	
Hints	
Comments	

Decryption Key

A	B	C	D	E	F	G	H	I	J	K	L	M
N	O	P	Q	R	S	T	U	V	W	X	Y	Z

(letter above equals below, and vice versa)

Cache Name	
Cache#	
Coordinates Lat	
Coordinates Lon	
Date Found	
Notes	
Hints	
Comments	

Cache Name	
Cache#	
Coordinates Lat	
Coordinates Lon	
Date Found	
Notes	
Hints	
Comments	

Decryption Key

A	B	C	D	E	F	G	H	I	J	K	L	M
N	O	P	Q	R	S	T	U	V	W	X	Y	Z

(letter above equals below, and vice versa)

Cache Name	
Cache#	
Coordinates Lat	
Coordinates Lon	
Date Found	
Notes	
Hints	
Comments	

Cache Name	
Cache#	
Coordinates Lat	
Coordinates Lon	
Date Found	
Notes	
Hints	
Comments	

Decryption Key

A	B	C	D	E	F	G	H	I	J	K	L	M
N	O	P	Q	R	S	T	U	V	W	X	Y	Z

(letter above equals below, and vice versa)

Cache Name	
Cache#	
Coordinates Lat	
Coordinates Lon	
Date Found	
Notes	
Hints	
Comments	

Cache Name	
Cache#	
Coordinates Lat	
Coordinates Lon	
Date Found	
Notes	
Hints	
Comments	

Decryption Key

A	B	C	D	E	F	G	H	I	J	K	L	M
N	O	P	Q	R	S	T	U	V	W	X	Y	Z

(letter above equals below, and vice versa)

Cache Name	
Cache#	
Coordinates Lat	
Coordinates Lon	
Date Found	
Notes	
Hints	
Comments	

Cache Name	
Cache#	
Coordinates Lat	
Coordinates Lon	
Date Found	
Notes	
Hints	
Comments	

Decryption Key

A	B	C	D	E	F	G	H	I	J	K	L	M
N	O	P	Q	R	S	T	U	V	W	X	Y	Z

(letter above equals below, and vice versa)

Cache Name	
Cache#	
Coordinates Lat	
Coordinates Lon	
Date Found	
Notes	
Hints	
Comments	

Cache Name	
Cache#	
Coordinates Lat	
Coordinates Lon	
Date Found	
Notes	
Hints	
Comments	

Decryption Key

A	B	C	D	E	F	G	H	I	J	K	L	M
N	O	P	Q	R	S	T	U	V	W	X	Y	Z

(letter above equals below, and vice versa)

Cache Name	
Cache#	
Coordinates Lat	
Coordinates Lon	
Date Found	
Notes	
Hints	
Comments	

Cache Name	
Cache#	
Coordinates Lat	
Coordinates Lon	
Date Found	
Notes	
Hints	
Comments	

Decryption Key

A	B	C	D	E	F	G	H	I	J	K	L	M
N	O	P	Q	R	S	T	U	V	W	X	Y	Z

(letter above equals below, and vice versa)

Cache Name	
Cache#	
Coordinates Lat	
Coordinates Lon	
Date Found	
Notes	
Hints	
Comments	

Cache Name	
Cache#	
Coordinates Lat	
Coordinates Lon	
Date Found	
Notes	
Hints	
Comments	

Decryption Key

A	B	C	D	E	F	G	H	I	J	K	L	M
N	O	P	Q	R	S	T	U	V	W	X	Y	Z

(letter above equals below, and vice versa)

Cache Name	
Cache#	
Coordinates Lat	
Coordinates Lon	
Date Found	
Notes	
Hints	
Comments	

Cache Name	
Cache#	
Coordinates Lat	
Coordinates Lon	
Date Found	
Notes	
Hints	
Comments	

Decryption Key

A	B	C	D	E	F	G	H	I	J	K	L	M
N	O	P	Q	R	S	T	U	V	W	X	Y	Z

(letter above equals below, and vice versa)

Cache Name	
Cache#	
Coordinates Lat	
Coordinates Lon	
Date Found	
Notes	
Hints	
Comments	

Cache Name	
Cache#	
Coordinates Lat	
Coordinates Lon	
Date Found	
Notes	
Hints	
Comments	

Decryption Key

A	B	C	D	E	F	G	H	I	J	K	L	M
N	O	P	Q	R	S	T	U	V	W	X	Y	Z

(letter above equals below, and vice versa)

Cache Name	
Cache#	
Coordinates Lat	
Coordinates Lon	
Date Found	
Notes	
Hints	
Comments	

Cache Name	
Cache#	
Coordinates Lat	
Coordinates Lon	
Date Found	
Notes	
Hints	
Comments	

Decryption Key

A	B	C	D	E	F	G	H	I	J	K	L	M
N	O	P	Q	R	S	T	U	V	W	X	Y	Z

(letter above equals below, and vice versa)

Cache Name	
Cache#	
Coordinates Lat	
Coordinates Lon	
Date Found	
Notes	
Hints	
Comments	

Cache Name	
Cache#	
Coordinates Lat	
Coordinates Lon	
Date Found	
Notes	
Hints	
Comments	

Decryption Key

A	B	C	D	E	F	G	H	I	J	K	L	M
N	O	P	Q	R	S	T	U	V	W	X	Y	Z

(letter above equals below, and vice versa)

Cache Name	
Cache#	
Coordinates Lat	
Coordinates Lon	
Date Found	
Notes	
Hints	
Comments	

Cache Name	
Cache#	
Coordinates Lat	
Coordinates Lon	
Date Found	
Notes	
Hints	
Comments	

Decryption Key

A	B	C	D	E	F	G	H	I	J	K	L	M
N	O	P	Q	R	S	T	U	V	W	X	Y	Z

(letter above equals below, and vice versa)

Cache Name	
Cache#	
Coordinates Lat	
Coordinates Lon	
Date Found	
Notes	
Hints	
Comments	

Cache Name	
Cache#	
Coordinates Lat	
Coordinates Lon	
Date Found	
Notes	
Hints	
Comments	

Decryption Key

A	B	C	D	E	F	G	H	I	J	K	L	M
N	O	P	Q	R	S	T	U	V	W	X	Y	Z

(letter above equals below, and vice versa)

Cache Name	
Cache#	
Coordinates Lat	
Coordinates Lon	
Date Found	
Notes	
Hints	
Comments	

Cache Name	
Cache#	
Coordinates Lat	
Coordinates Lon	
Date Found	
Notes	
Hints	
Comments	

Decryption Key

A	B	C	D	E	F	G	H	I	J	K	L	M
N	O	P	Q	R	S	T	U	V	W	X	Y	Z

(letter above equals below, and vice versa)

Cache Name	
Cache#	
Coordinates Lat	
Coordinates Lon	
Date Found	
Notes	
Hints	
Comments	

Cache Name	
Cache#	
Coordinates Lat	
Coordinates Lon	
Date Found	
Notes	
Hints	
Comments	

Decryption Key

A	B	C	D	E	F	G	H	I	J	K	L	M
N	O	P	Q	R	S	T	U	V	W	X	Y	Z

(letter above equals below, and vice versa)

Cache Name	
Cache#	
Coordinates Lat	
Coordinates Lon	
Date Found	
Notes	
Hints	
Comments	

Cache Name	
Cache#	
Coordinates Lat	
Coordinates Lon	
Date Found	
Notes	
Hints	
Comments	

Decryption Key

A	B	C	D	E	F	G	H	I	J	K	L	M
N	O	P	Q	R	S	T	U	V	W	X	Y	Z

(letter above equals below, and vice versa)

Cache Name	
Cache#	
Coordinates Lat	
Coordinates Lon	
Date Found	
Notes	
Hints	
Comments	

Cache Name	
Cache#	
Coordinates Lat	
Coordinates Lon	
Date Found	
Notes	
Hints	
Comments	

Decryption Key

A	B	C	D	E	F	G	H	I	J	K	L	M
N	O	P	Q	R	S	T	U	V	W	X	Y	Z

(letter above equals below, and vice versa)

Cache Name	
Cache#	
Coordinates Lat	
Coordinates Lon	
Date Found	
Notes	
Hints	
Comments	

Cache Name	
Cache#	
Coordinates Lat	
Coordinates Lon	
Date Found	
Notes	
Hints	
Comments	

Decryption Key

A	B	C	D	E	F	G	H	I	J	K	L	M
N	O	P	Q	R	S	T	U	V	W	X	Y	Z

(letter above equals below, and vice versa)

Geocaching

Cache Name	
Cache#	
Coordinates Lat	
Coordinates Lon	
Date Found	
Notes	
Hints	
Comments	

Cache Name	
Cache#	
Coordinates Lat	
Coordinates Lon	
Date Found	
Notes	
Hints	
Comments	

Decryption Key

A	B	C	D	E	F	G	H	I	J	K	L	M
N	O	P	Q	R	S	T	U	V	W	X	Y	Z

(letter above equals below, and vice versa)

Cache Name	
Cache#	
Coordinates Lat	
Coordinates Lon	
Date Found	
Notes	
Hints	
Comments	

Cache Name	
Cache#	
Coordinates Lat	
Coordinates Lon	
Date Found	
Notes	
Hints	
Comments	

Decryption Key

A	B	C	D	E	F	G	H	I	J	K	L	M
N	O	P	Q	R	S	T	U	V	W	X	Y	Z

(letter above equals below, and vice versa)

Cache Name	
Cache#	
Coordinates Lat	
Coordinates Lon	
Date Found	
Notes	
Hints	
Comments	

Cache Name	
Cache#	
Coordinates Lat	
Coordinates Lon	
Date Found	
Notes	
Hints	
Comments	

Decryption Key

A	B	C	D	E	F	G	H	I	J	K	L	M
N	O	P	Q	R	S	T	U	V	W	X	Y	Z

(letter above equals below, and vice versa)

Cache Name	
Cache#	
Coordinates Lat	
Coordinates Lon	
Date Found	
Notes	
Hints	
Comments	

Cache Name	
Cache#	
Coordinates Lat	
Coordinates Lon	
Date Found	
Notes	
Hints	
Comments	

Decryption Key

A	B	C	D	E	F	G	H	I	J	K	L	M
N	O	P	Q	R	S	T	U	V	W	X	Y	Z

(letter above equals below, and vice versa)

Cache Name	
Cache#	
Coordinates Lat	
Coordinates Lon	
Date Found	
Notes	
Hints	
Comments	

Cache Name	
Cache#	
Coordinates Lat	
Coordinates Lon	
Date Found	
Notes	
Hints	
Comments	

Decryption Key

A	B	C	D	E	F	G	H	I	J	K	L	M
N	O	P	Q	R	S	T	U	V	W	X	Y	Z

(letter above equals below, and vice versa)

Cache Name	
Cache#	
Coordinates Lat	
Coordinates Lon	
Date Found	
Notes	
Hints	
Comments	

Cache Name	
Cache#	
Coordinates Lat	
Coordinates Lon	
Date Found	
Notes	
Hints	
Comments	

Decryption Key

A	B	C	D	E	F	G	H	I	J	K	L	M
N	O	P	Q	R	S	T	U	V	W	X	Y	Z

(letter above equals below, and vice versa)

Geocaching

Cache Name	
Cache#	
Coordinates Lat	
Coordinates Lon	
Date Found	
Notes	
Hints	
Comments	

Cache Name	
Cache#	
Coordinates Lat	
Coordinates Lon	
Date Found	
Notes	
Hints	
Comments	

Decryption Key

A	B	C	D	E	F	G	H	I	J	K	L	M
N	O	P	Q	R	S	T	U	V	W	X	Y	Z

(letter above equals below, and vice versa)

Cache Name	
Cache#	
Coordinates Lat	
Coordinates Lon	
Date Found	
Notes	
Hints	
Comments	

Cache Name	
Cache#	
Coordinates Lat	
Coordinates Lon	
Date Found	
Notes	
Hints	
Comments	

Decryption Key

A	B	C	D	E	F	G	H	I	J	K	L	M
N	O	P	Q	R	S	T	U	V	W	X	Y	Z

(letter above equals below, and vice versa)

Cache Name	
Cache#	
Coordinates Lat	
Coordinates Lon	
Date Found	
Notes	
Hints	
Comments	

Cache Name	
Cache#	
Coordinates Lat	
Coordinates Lon	
Date Found	
Notes	
Hints	
Comments	

Decryption Key

A	B	C	D	E	F	G	H	I	J	K	L	M
N	O	P	Q	R	S	T	U	V	W	X	Y	Z

(letter above equals below, and vice versa)

Cache Name	
Cache#	
Coordinates Lat	
Coordinates Lon	
Date Found	
Notes	
Hints	
Comments	

Cache Name	
Cache#	
Coordinates Lat	
Coordinates Lon	
Date Found	
Notes	
Hints	
Comments	

Decryption Key

A	B	C	D	E	F	G	H	I	J	K	L	M
N	O	P	Q	R	S	T	U	V	W	X	Y	Z

(letter above equals below, and vice versa)

Geocaching

Cache Name	
Cache#	
Coordinates Lat	
Coordinates Lon	
Date Found	
Notes	
Hints	
Comments	

Cache Name	
Cache#	
Coordinates Lat	
Coordinates Lon	
Date Found	
Notes	
Hints	
Comments	

Decryption Key

A	B	C	D	E	F	G	H	I	J	K	L	M
N	O	P	Q	R	S	T	U	V	W	X	Y	Z

(letter above equals below, and vice versa)

Cache Name	
Cache#	
Coordinates Lat	
Coordinates Lon	
Date Found	
Notes	
Hints	
Comments	

Cache Name	
Cache#	
Coordinates Lat	
Coordinates Lon	
Date Found	
Notes	
Hints	
Comments	

Decryption Key

A	B	C	D	E	F	G	H	I	J	K	L	M
N	O	P	Q	R	S	T	U	V	W	X	Y	Z

(letter above equals below, and vice versa)

Cache Name	
Cache#	
Coordinates Lat	
Coordinates Lon	
Date Found	
Notes	
Hints	
Comments	

Cache Name	
Cache#	
Coordinates Lat	
Coordinates Lon	
Date Found	
Notes	
Hints	
Comments	

Decryption Key

A	B	C	D	E	F	G	H	I	J	K	L	M
N	O	P	Q	R	S	T	U	V	W	X	Y	Z

(letter above equals below, and vice versa)

Made in the USA
Middletown, DE
17 December 2016